Mercury and the woodman

Story written by Abbie Rushton
Illustrated by Tim Archbold

Speed Sounds

Ask your child to say the sounds (not the letter names) clearly and quickly, in and out of order. Make sure he or she does not add 'uh' to the end of the sounds, e.g. 'f' not 'fuh'.

Each box contains one sound. Focus sounds for this story are circled.

Consonants

f	l	m	n	r	s	v	z	sh	th	ng
ff	ll	mm	nn	rr	ss	**ve**	zz			nk
ph	**le**	mb	kn	wr	se		se			
			gn		c		s			
					ce					

b	c	d	g	h	j	p	qu	t	w	x	y	ch
bb	k	dd	gg		g	pp		tt	wh			**tch**
	ck		gu		ge							
					dge							

Vowels

Ask your child to say the sounds in and out of order.

a	e	i	o	u	ay	ee	igh	ow
	ea				a-e	ea	i-e	o-e
					a	y	ie	o
						e	i	oe
at	hen	in	on	up	day	see	high	blow

oo	oo	ar	or	air	ir	ou	oy
u-e			oor	are	ur	ow	oi
ue			ore		er		
			aw				
zoo	look	car	for	fair	whirl	shout	boy

Story Green Words

For each word ask your child to read the separate sounds, e.g. 'b-u-s', 'p-oo-l' and then blend sounds together to make the word, e.g. 'bus', 'pool'. Sometimes one sound is represented by more than one letter, e.g. 'th', 'oo'. These are underlined.

tale shame voice wept axe* gone*

Ask children to say the syllables and then read the whole word.

grate|ful dis|may wood|man Flo|rin a|loft res|ponse la|zy

Mer|cur|y sil|ver gold|en*

Ask children to read the root first and then the whole word with the suffix.

fade → fading wade → waded proud → proudly

display → displaying glow → glowing tempt → tempted

behave → behaved vanish → vanished

* *Challenge Words*

Vocabulary Check

Tell your child the meaning of each word in the context of the story.

	definition:	**sentence:**
wept	*cried*	*Florin wept in dismay.*
dismay	*worry*	*Florin wept in dismay.*
tempted	*wanted something he shouldn't*	*Florin was tempted to take it.*
longingly	*wanting something a lot*	*Florin looked at the axe longingly.*
tossed	*threw*	*The next day he went to the lake, tossed in his axe and wept loudly.*
aloft	*up high*	*As he leant out to grab the axe, Mercury held it aloft.*
in shame	*unhappily as he had done something wrong*	*The lazy woodman hung his head in shame.*
waded	*walked through water*	*The lazy woodman... waded into the lake to look for his axe.*

Red Words

Red words don't sound like they look. Ask your child to read the words but if he or she gets stuck read the word to your child.

would	by	one	other
my	once	through	all
old	your	are	who
son	two	call	water
does	were	over	once

Mercury and the woodman

Do not read the story to your child first. Point to the words as your child reads. If your child gets stuck on a word help him or her say the sounds and blend them together. Re-read each sentence to your child to help him or her remember what he or she has read. Discuss what is happening on each page.

This is the tale of a poor woodman called Florin.
He had been chopping wood all day by the lake.
The light was fading and the shadows were long.

Suddenly, Florin's hand slipped, and
his axe fell into the lake.

Florin wept in dismay. "My axe!
I will starve without wood to sell."

“All is not lost,” said a soft voice. Florin gazed at the man who was suddenly before him. “You are... Mercury! The god Mercury!”

“I will help you,” Mercury said.
Then he swam to the bottom of the lake.

When Mercury came back, Florin gasped. Mercury held a glowing, golden axe!
Florin was tempted to take it.
But he shook his head. “I wish it were my axe,” he said sadly, “but it is not.”

Once more, Mercury swam to the bottom of the lake.

When the god came back, Florin gulped. Mercury held a sparkling, silver axe. Florin looked at the axe longingly.

But he shook his head. "I wish it were my axe," he said sadly, "but it is not."

Once more, Mercury swam to the bottom of the lake.

When the god came back, Florin jumped for joy. Mercury held a simple, wooden axe. “My axe! My trusty axe!” he said. “Thank you. I am so grateful!”

“You have behaved well, Florin,” said Mercury. “You may keep the gold and silver axes too.” Florin stood still in shock.

Just as Florin was about to thank him, Mercury vanished.

Florin raced away to tell the other woodmen of his luck. "Look!" he said, proudly displaying his three axes.

One of the woodmen started to grumble, "It's not fair that Florin has all the luck."

This lazy woodman came up with a plan. The next day he went to the lake, tossed in his axe and wept loudly. "My axe! I will starve without wood to sell."

Just as before, Mercury came. “I will help you,” he said.

Once more, Mercury swam to the bottom of the lake and came back with a glowing, golden axe.

“My axe! My trusty axe!” said the lazy woodman. As he leant out to grab the axe, Mercury held it aloft.

“This is not yours,” Mercury said. “You have behaved badly so I will not fetch your axe.”

The lazy woodman hung his head in shame. "I am sorry, but I still need my axe. Will you help me?"

As he looked up, Mercury vanished.
"Mercury...? *Mercury?*" the lazy woodman shouted. But Mercury had gone.

The lazy woodman sighed, took off his boots and waded into the lake to look for his axe.

Now ask your child to re-read the story helping him or her think about the best way to read each sentence.

Questions to talk about

Read the questions aloud to your child and ask him or her to find the answers on the relevant pages. Do not ask your child to read the questions – the words are harder than he or she can read at the moment.

p.9 How did Florin feel when he dropped his axe?

p.10 Which god came to help?

p.10 Mercury brought Florin a glowing axe. What was it made of?

p.12 Why did Florin jump for joy?

p.13 Why did the lazy woodman toss his axe in the lake?

p.14 The lazy woodman tried to grab the golden axe. What did Mercury do?

p.15 What lesson did the lazy woodman learn?

Questions to read and answer

Ask your child to read the questions and find the correct answer in the story.

1. Florin was **a god / a doctor / a woodman**.

2. Florin met Mercury **in a house / by the lake / in the hills**.

3. Mercury said Florin could keep **two axes / the wooden axe / all the axes**.

4. The lazy woodman said he would **be rich / starve / feel sad** without wood to sell.

5. The lazy woodman **had to look for his axe / was given an axe / did not need an axe.**

Speedy Green Words

Ask your child to read the words clearly and quickly – across the rows, down the columns, and in and out of order.

day	help	look	swam
sighed	more	may	need
shouted	joy	started	poor
away	wood	head	sorry
light	without	about	came